Jerrin Thomas Panachakel

A Textbook on Microcontroller Based System Design using 8051
and ARM

Jerrin Thomas Panachakel

A Textbook on Microcontroller Based System Design using 8051 and ARM

LAP LAMBERT Academic Publishing

Impressum / Imprint
Bibliografische Information der Deutschen Nationalbibliothek: Die Deutsche Nationalbibliothek verzeichnet diese Publikation in der Deutschen Nationalbibliografie; detaillierte bibliografische Daten sind im Internet über http://dnb.d-nb.de abrufbar.
Alle in diesem Buch genannten Marken und Produktnamen unterliegen warenzeichen-, marken- oder patentrechtlichem Schutz bzw. sind Warenzeichen oder eingetragene Warenzeichen der jeweiligen Inhaber. Die Wiedergabe von Marken, Produktnamen, Gebrauchsnamen, Handelsnamen, Warenbezeichnungen u.s.w. in diesem Werk berechtigt auch ohne besondere Kennzeichnung nicht zu der Annahme, dass solche Namen im Sinne der Warenzeichen- und Markenschutzgesetzgebung als frei zu betrachten wären und daher von jedermann benutzt werden dürften.

Bibliographic information published by the Deutsche Nationalbibliothek: The Deutsche Nationalbibliothek lists this publication in the Deutsche Nationalbibliografie; detailed bibliographic data are available in the Internet at http://dnb.d-nb.de.
Any brand names and product names mentioned in this book are subject to trademark, brand or patent protection and are trademarks or registered trademarks of their respective holders. The use of brand names, product names, common names, trade names, product descriptions etc. even without a particular marking in this work is in no way to be construed to mean that such names may be regarded as unrestricted in respect of trademark and brand protection legislation and could thus be used by anyone.

Coverbild / Cover image: www.ingimage.com

Verlag / Publisher:
LAP LAMBERT Academic Publishing
ist ein Imprint der / is a trademark of
OmniScriptum GmbH & Co. KG
Heinrich-Böcking-Str. 6-8, 66121 Saarbrücken, Deutschland / Germany
Email: info@lap-publishing.com

Herstellung: siehe letzte Seite /
Printed at: see last page
ISBN: 978-3-659-69217-8

A Textbook
on

Microcontroller Based System Design using 8051 and ARM

Jerrin Thomas Panachakel

Research Associate
Dept. of Electrical Engineering
Indian Institute of Science, Bangalore, India

jerrin.panachakel[at]mile.ee.iisc.ernet.in
jerrin.panachakel[at]gmail.com

Acknowledgement

I wish to place on record my deepest gratitude to all my teachers, especially **Prof. Viswanatha Rao** (Professor & Vice Principal, MBCET, Trivandrum, India), my beloved Rao sir, a true *guru* and a pioneer in embedded systems, who taught me microcontroller based system design in the under-graduate level. I thank my mentor, **Prof. A. G. Ramakrishnan** (Professor, IISc, Bangalore), for the motivation and support he extended. He has always surprised me with his diligence and knowledge. I am thankful **Dr. Jiji C.V.** (Professor, CET, Trivandrum, India), for his guidance. His passion to teach and ability to inspire has always moved us. I am indebted to **Ms. Linu Shine** (Assistant Professor, CET, Trivandrum), India, who taught me embedded systems in the post-graduate level. I thank all my friends, especially **Ms. Lakshmi Mohan Vijaya**, without whose support, I couldn't have had completed this.

I am grateful to **Prof. Baiju Sasidharan** (co-ordinator, Step4U Scholar Support Programme, CET, Trivandrum), for giving me an oppurtunity to be a part of the programme. It was **Mr. Nithin R.B.** (Ph.D. Scholar, CET, Trivandrum, India) who recommended my name to Prof. Baiju Sasidharan. I am deeply indebted to him.

I am grateful to my dear students.

This lecture notes was prepared based on several resources including "The 8051 Microcontroller and Embedded Systems Using Assembly and C", by Muhammad Ali Mazidi, Janice Gillispie Mazidi & Rolin D. McKinlay, "ARM System Developer's Guide: Designing and Optimizing System Software " by Andrew Sloss, Dominic Symes & Chris Wright and the presentation on "Introduction to Computing", by Chung-Ping Young. I am grateful to the developers of these resources.

Jerrin Thomas Panachakel

To my acha and amma.

Contents

Chapter 1

Assembly Language Programming: I

1.1 Addressing Modes

The process of writing program for the microcontroller mainly consists of giving instructions (commands) in the specific order in which they should be executed in order to carry out a specific task. An instruction typically consists of two parts,

- *Operation:* The action that needs to be performed.

- *Operand:* The data on which the action should be performed.

For example, consider the following assembly language instruction,

```
ADD A,B;        A=A+B
```

Here, the operation to be performed is *addition* and the operands are the contents of registers *A & B*.

The various methods of accessing the operands are called **addressing modes**. The 8051 supports a total of five distinct addressing modes. They are,

1. immediate

2. register

3. direct

4. register indirect

5. indexed

1.2 Immediate addressing mode

- Named so become when the instruction is assembled, the operand comes immediately after the opcode (operation code).

- The source operand is a constant.

- The immediate data must be preceded by the pound sign, #

Examples:

```
MOV A, #12H      ;A=12H
MOV R6, #22H     ;R6=22H
MOV DPTR, #1121H ;DPTR=1121H
MOV DPH, #25H;   ;DPH=25H
```

1.3 Register addressing mode

- The registers are used to hold the data.

Examples:

```
MOV A,R3    ;copy the contents of R3 to A
ADD A,B     ;add the contents of B to A
```

The following instructions will produce error,

```
MOV DPTR, A  ;source and destination  are of different sizes
MOV R3,R4    ;movement of data between Rn registers
```

In these two modes, data is either tagged along with the instruction or is available in one of the registers. But practically, the data to be processed will be in some memory location of RAM or in the code space of ROM. The addressing modes discussed below allows us to access these data.

1.4 Direct addressing mode

In the direct addressing mode, the data is in the RAM memory location whose address is known and this address is given as a part of the instruction. Examples:

```
MOV R0,40H    ;save content of RAM location 40H in R0
MOV 56H,A     ;save content of A in RAM location 56H
MOV 7,2       ;copy R2 to R7
MOV 0E0H,R2   ;copy R2 to A
```

2

1.5 Register indirect addressing mode

- A register is used as a pointer to the data.

- If the data is inside the CPU, only registers R0 and R1 are used for this purpose.

- When registers are used as pointers, they must be preceded by the "@" symbol.

- Use os register indirect addressing mode makes it accessing data dynamic rather than staticas in the case of direct addressing mode.

Examples:

```
MOV A, @R0      ;move the contents of RAM location whose
                ;address is held by R) into A
MOV @R1, AB     ;move the contents of B into the RAM location
                ;whose  address is held by R1
```

1.6 Indexed addressing mode

- Usually used for accessing data elements of look-up table entries located in the program ROM space of 8051.

- The instruction used for this purpose is "MOVC A, @A+DPTR"

Example:

```
ORG 0000H
MOV DPTR, #0400H
MOVC A, @A+DPTR
HERE: SJAMP HERE
ORG 400H
DB "S"
END
```

3

Instruction	Opcode	Bytes	Cycles
MOVC A,@A +DPTR	93H	1	2

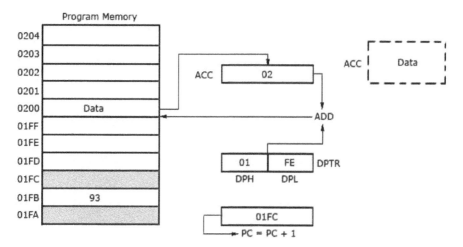

Figure 1.1: Indexed addressing *source:* http://www.circuitstoday.com/8051-addressing-modes

1.7 Assembly Language Programs

1.7.1 Addition of 8 bit numbers

Q. Write an ALP to add 30H and 44H and store the result in R2

```
MOV A,#30H
MOV B,#44H
ADD A,B
MOV R2,A
```

Q. Write an ALP to fetch data from RAM memory locations 40H and 41H ans store their sum in 55H

```
MOV A,40H
MOV B,41H
ADD A,B
MOV 55H,A
```

4

Q. R0 and R1 contains the RAM memory locations two elements. Write an ALP to find the sum of the two elements ans store the result in the memory location pointed by R3

```
MOV A,@R0
MOV B,@R1
ADD A,B
MOV 0,3
MOV @R0,A
```

1.7.2 Addition of 16 bit numbers

Q. Write an ALP to add the 16bit numbers 1444H and 22DBH. Store the lower-byte of the result in R3, upper byte in R2 and carry, if any, in R1.

```
;Load the first value into R6 and R7
MOV R6,#1Ah
MOV R7,#44h

;Load the second value into R4 and R5
MOV R4,#22h
MOV R5,#0DBh
;Step 1 of the process
MOV A,R7      ;Move the low-byte into the accumulator
ADD A,R5      ;Add the second low-byte to the accumulator
MOV R3,A      ;Move the answer to the low-byte of the result

;Step 2 of the process
MOV A,R6      ;Move the high-byte into the accumulator
ADDC A,R4     ;Add the 2nd high-byte to A plus carry.
MOV R2,A      ;Move the answer to the high-byte of the result

;Step 3 of the process
MOV A,#00h    ;By default, the highest byte will be zero.
ADDC A,#00h   ;Add zero, plus carry from step 2.
MOV  R1,A     ;Move the answer to the highest byte of  the result
```

1.7.3 Others

Q. Write an ALP to see if register A has en even number. If so, make it odd.

```
    JB ACC.0, ND
    INC A
ND: SJMP ND
```

Q. Memory location 4404H and 4405H contains the upper and lower bytes of a 16bit number. Similarly, 3303H and 3304H contains another 16 bit number. Wrtie an ALP to add the two numbers and store the results in R3 and R4. If there is carry, make the accumulator value 0FFH.

Q. Factorial of an 8-bit number

```
       MOV R0,71H
       MOV A,#01
HERE:  MOV B,R0
       MUL AB
       DJNZ R0,HERE
```

Q. Write an ALP to sum the elements in an array

```
       MOV DPTR,#4400
       CLR C
       MOV R0,#00H
       MOV R1,#00H
ADDIT: MOVX A,@DPTR
       MOV B,A
       MOV A,R0
       ADDC A,B
       MOV R0,A
       JNC NC
       INC R1
NC:    INC DPTR
       SJMP ADDIT
```

Chapter 2

Assembly Language Programming: II

2.1 GCD and LCM

Q. Write an ALP to find the Greatest Common Divisor (GCD) of two numbers using Euclid's algorithm and hence find their Least Common Multiple (LCM)

2.1.1 Euclid's algorithm and LCM from GCD

Given two integers a and b, then,

- $GCD(a, b) = GCD(b, a \mod b)$

- Continue the above recursive operation until the value of the 2nd term is zero. The value of the first term when the second is zero will be the GCD of the pair of given numbers, since $DGCD(a, 0) = a$.

- $GCD(145, 30) = GCD(30, 25) = GCD(25, 5) = GCD(5, 0) = 5$

- $LCM(a, b) = \frac{a \times b}{GCD(a,b)}$

- Flowchart given in Fig. 2.1.

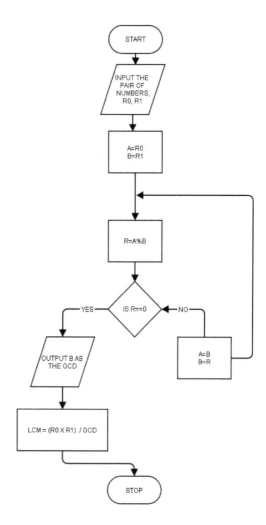

Figure 2.1: Flowchart: GCD and LCM

2.1.2 ALP

```
        MOV R0,#22
        MOV R1,#11
        MOV A,R0
        MOV B,R1
LAB:    MOV R3,B
        DIV AB
        MOV A,B
        JZ LAB2
        MOV A,R3
        SJMP LAB
LAB2:   SJMP LAB2
```

2.2 Sorting of elements in an array

2.2.1 Swapping of consecutive elements in an array

Q. Write an ALP to swap the consecutive elements in an array. The starting address of the array is stored in the register R4 and the number of elements in stored in R5.

Pseudocode

1. R5=no. of elements

2. R4= add. of the first element

3. Decrement R5

4. Repeat

    R0=R4

    Increment R4

    R1=R4

    A=@R0

    B=@R1

    SWAP A & B

    Decrement R5

5. Until R5==0

9

ALP

```
        DEC R5
LAB2:   MOV 0H,4H
        INC R4
        MOV 1H,4H
        MOV A,@R0
        MOV B,@R1
        MOV @R1,A
        MOV @R0,B
        DJNZ R5,LAB2
```

2.2.2 Magnitude Comparison

Q. Write an ALP to compare the magnitudes of two numbers stored in A and B and store the highest number in R0. If both the integers are same, store the number in R1.

HINT: Use *CJNZ A,B,addr.* *CJNZ* affects the CY flag.

2.2.3 Sorting

Q. Write an ALP to sort the elements in an array in the descending order. The address of the first element in stored in *R7* and the number of elements in stored in *R6*.

```
      MOV R6,#9; NUMBER OF ELEMENTS
      MOV R7, #70H; ADD. OF FIRST ELEMENT

LAB3:MOV 5H,6H; BACK-UP OF NO. OF ELE.
      MOV 4H,7H; BACK-UP OF ADD. OF FIRST ELE.
      DEC R5
LAB2:MOV 0H,4H
      INC R4
      MOV 1H,4H
      MOV A,@R0
      MOV B,@R1
      CJNE A,B,LAB1
LAB1:JNC NSWP
      MOV @R1,A
      MOV @R0,B
NSWP: DJNZ R5,LAB2
      DJNZ R6,LAB3
```

2.3   Fibonacci Series

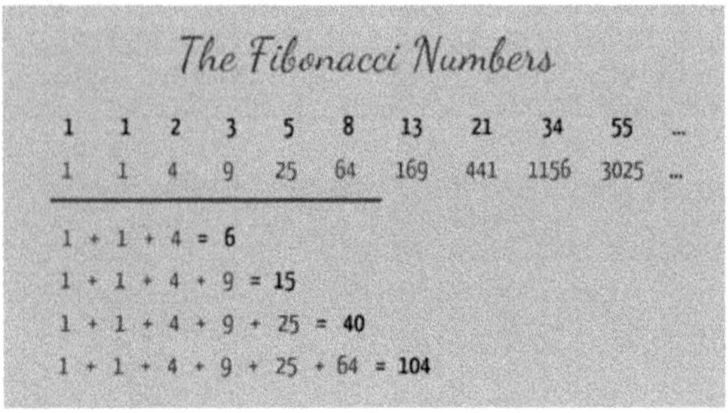

Figure 2.2: Fibonacci numbers

```
MOV 70H,#00
MOV 71H,#01
MOV R1,#00
MOV R3,#10
DEC R3
DEC R3
MOV R0,#70H
LAB: MOV A,@R0
INC R0
MOV B,@R0
ADD A,B
INC R0
MOV @R0,A
DEC R0
DJNZ R3, LAB
```

Q. Write a program that finds the number of ones in a given byte

[May 2012, KU]

```
    MOV DPTR,#4410H; assuming that the data is in location 4410H
    MOV A,@DPTR
    MOV R2,#8
    MOV R1,#0
    CLR C
LP: RLC A
    JNC LAB
    INC R1
LAB: DJNZ R2, LP
```

11

Chapter 3

8051 Timer and Counter Programming

3.1   Introduction

8051 has two on-chip timers which can be used for,

1. Keeping time and/or calculating time between events

2. Providing time delay between two executions

3. Counting the occurrence of events

4. Generating baud rates for serial communication

Other than using on-chip timers, which uses both hardware and software for their working, these four requirements can be achieved using,

- Pure hardware, for instance, by using a 555 timer or

- By pure software, for instance by using the following code

```
MOV R0,#255; 2 machine cycles
HERE: DJNZ R0,HERE; 255 machine cycles
```

where the total delay will be 255 × 1 clock period

What us bad with the above two approaches is that the former lacks flexibility, that is, if we are using a 555 timer, we have to change the resistors and/or capacitors to change the frequency. Also, there will be an error in the frequency generated due to the tolerance associated with the components used and also due to the changes in component value due to ageing, temperature and humidity variations etc. In the latter approach, though it is highly flexible, the processor is "tied down" and it cannot do any other job at that time.

By using the on-chip timer, we achieve enough flexibility and accuracy and at the same time, the processor isn't tied down; it can do some other useful works at the same time.

3.2 Timer Registers

3.2.1 TimerX register

- As mentioned earlier, there are two on-chip timers in 8051 *Timer 1 & Timer 0*, both of which are 16−bit timers.

- Since 8051 has an 8−bit architecture, almost all user accessible registers are 8−bit wide. Therefore, each timer has two 8−bit registers associated with them, one for storing the lower byte and the other for storing the upper byte. (See Fig. 3.1)

- The lower byte register of timer 1 is called **TL0** (**T**imer **0**, **L**ower byte). The upper byte is stored in **TH0**.

- These registers can be accessed like any other registers. For example, *MOV TH0,#22H* moves *22H* into *TH0*. Similarly, *MOV R0,TL0* moves the contents of *TL0* into *R0*.

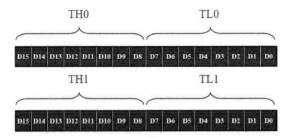

Figure 3.1: *TH* and *TL* registers

3.2.2 TMOD register

- TMOD or **T**imer **MOD**e is used to set the various timer operating mode.

- Both timer 0 and timer 1 shares the same register, as shown in Fig. 3.2.

- TMOD register is **NOT BIT ADDRESSABLE**

13

Figure 3.2: *TH* and *TL* registers

GATE

- When the GATE pin is 1 (set), the timer/counter is enabled only when the *INTx* pin is high and the *TRx* control bit of the **TCON** register is set.

- When the GATE pin is cleared, the timer is enabled whenever the *TRx* control bit is set.

$C/\bar{T}$

- To select between counter operation and timer operation.

- When set, the timer will operate in the event counter mode, i.e., the events will be input through the *Tx* input pin.

- When cleared, the timer will operate in the delay generator mode/the timer mode. The clock source will be the system clock.

M0 and M1

- To select the mode of operation.

- The different modes are shown in Table 3.1.

Table 3.1: Timer modes

M1	M0	*Mode*	Operating Mode
0	0	0	13-bit timer mode THx: 8-bit timer/counter TLx: 5-bit presclaer
0	1	1	16-bit timer mode
1	0	2	8-bit auto reload TLx: counter THx: value to be reloaded when TLx overflows
1	1	3	Split timer mode

14

Clock frequency of the timer

- The frequency of the timer will be $\frac{1}{12}^{th}$ the frequency of the clock. That is, if the clock frequency is $1MHz$ then the timer frequency will be 1MHz.

Exercise

Exercise 3.1 *Indicate which mode and which timer are selected for each of the following. (a) MOV TMOD, #01H (b) MOV TMOD, #20H (c) MOV TMOD, #12H*

Solution:

(a) TMOD = 00000001, mode 1 of timer 0 is selected.

(b) TMOD = 00100000, mode 2 of timer 1 is selected.

(c) TMOD = 00010010, mode 2 of timer 0, and mode 1 of timer 1 are selected.

3.2.3 TCON register

| TF1 | TR1 | TF0 | TR0 | IE1 | IT1 | IE0 | IT0 |

Figure 3.3: TCON register

- TCON ot **T**imer/Counter **CON**trol register is shown in Fig. 3.3.

- It is a bit addressable register.

  TF1 or **TCON.7**: Timer 1 overflow flag. Set by the hardware when the Timer/Counter overflows. Cleared by hardware as processor vectors to the interrupt service routine

  TR1 or **TCON.6**: Timer 1 run control bit. Set/cleared by the software to turn Timer/Counter 1 ON/OFF.

  TF0 or **TCON.5**: Flag of Timer 0, similar to the TF1 of timer 1

  TR0 or **TCON.4**: Similar to the TR1 flag of timer 1.

  IE1 or **TCON.3**: External interrupt 1 edge flag. Set by hardware when External interrupt edge is detected. Cleared by hardware when interrupt is processed.

  IT1 or **TCON.2**: Interrupt 1 type control. Set/cleared by software to specify falling edge/low level triggered External interrupt.

  IE0 or **TCON.1**: Similar to IE1

  IT0 or **TCON.0**: Similar to IT1

3.3 Timer modes

3.3.1 Mode 0: 13 bit timer mode

- Mode 0 timer is a 13 bit timer, included in 8051 to make it compatible with its predecessor, 8048. Uses the 8 bits of THx and lower 5 bits of TLx.

- TLx acts as a 5 bit prescaler, or a modulo 32 prescaler.

- The timer can store only 8192 values and rolls over after 8192 machine cycles. With the unused bits set to 0, the maximum value the registers can store together is 1FFF H and rolls over to 0000 H after that and sets the TFx flag.

16

3.3.2 Mode 1: 16 bit timer mode

- In mode one, the range of values allowed are from 0000 H to FFFF H.

- With GATE=0, the timer can be started by setting the TR0 flag, for example, for starting timer 0, the instruction is *SETB TR0*.

- After the counter is started, it counts upto FFFF H.

- When the timer rolls over from FFFF H to 0000 H, the TFx flag will be set.

- For repeating the process, the registers THx and TLx must be reloaded with the original values as shown in Fig. 3.4.

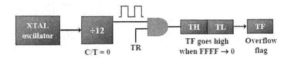

Figure 3.4: MODE 1

Exercise

Exercise 3.2 *Find the delay generated by Timer 0 in the following code*

```
       MOV TMOD, #01;  Timer 0, Mode 1
       MOV TL0, #3EH
       MOV TH0, #0B8H
       SET TR0
AGAIN:JNB TF0, AGAIN
       CLR TR0
       CLR TF0
```

Solution:
$FFFFH - 0B83EH + 1 = 47C2H = 18370D.$
Therefore, $delay = 18370 \times 1.085\mu s = 19.93145ms.$

Exercise

]

Exercise 3.3 *What is the delay if TH0= 0FF H and TL0 =00 H with XTAL=22 MHz*

Ans.: $139.3\mu s.$

17

Exercise

Exercise 3.4 *Find the frequency of the square wave generated by the following code. Assume XTAL=11.0592MHz*

```
HERE:MOV TMOD, #01; Timer 0, Mode 1
     MOV TL0, #F2H; 2 MC
     MOV TH0, #0FFH; 2 MC
     CPL P1.5; 1 MC
     ACALL DELAY; 2 MC
     SJMP HERE; 2 MC

DELAY:SET TR0; 1 MC
AGAIN:JNB TF0, AGAIN; 14 MC
     CLR TR0; 1MC
     CLR TF0; 1 MC
     RET; 2 MC
```

Solution:
$FFFFH - 0B83EH + 1 = 47C2H = 18370D$.
Therefore, $delay = 18370 \times 1.085\mu s = 19.93145ms$.

3.3.3 Steps to find the value to be loaded into the timer register

Let XTAL=x and the required delay=d. Then,

1. $n = \frac{d*x}{12}$

2. $v = max - n + 1$ where max is the maximum value of the timer before overflow.

3. Convert n to hex, let the result be $yyxx$.

4. $TL = xx$ and $TH = yy$

Q. Write an ALP to generate a time delay of 5ms using Timer 1 in mode 0.

```
        MOV TMOD,#01
HERE:   MOV TL0,#00H
        MOV TH0,#0EEH
        SETB TR0
AGAIN:JNB TF0,AGAIN
        CLR TR0
        CLR TF0
```

Q. Write an ALP to generate a rectangular wave with ON time of 3 ms and OFF time of 10 ms on all pins of port 0. Assume an XTAL of 22 MHz. Use Timer 0 in mode 1.

```
        MOV TMOD,#01H
BACK:   MOV TL0,#62H
        MOV TH0,#0B8H
        MOV P0,#00H
        ACALL DELAY
        MOV TL0,#84H
        MOV TH0,#0EAH
        MOV P0,#0FFH
        ACALL DELAY
        SJMP BACK
DELAY:SETB TR0
        JNB TF0,AGAIN
        CLR TR0
        CLR TF0
        RET
```

Q. Assuming XTAL of 22 MHz, write a program to generate a pulse train of 2 seconds time period on pin P2.4. Use timer 1 in mode 1.
Exceeds maximum delay possible (35.75ms). We need 1ms delay. So, we repeat the maximum delay 28 times.

```
        MOV TMOD,#01H
REPT:   MOV R0,#28
        CPL P2.4
BACK:   MOV TL1,#00H
        MOV TH1,#00H
        SETB TR1
AGAIN:JNB TF1,AGAIN
        CLR TR1
        CLR TF1
        DJNZ R0,BACK
        SJMP REPT
```

19

3.3.4 Mode 2: 8 bit auto reload mode

- 8 bit timer, so range of values is from 00H to FFH, i.e., the maximum value is 255.

- The initial value is loaded into the higher byte. A copy of the same is passed to the lower byte. The Timer can update from 00H to FFH. The Timer rolls over from FFH to initial value automatically as shown in Fig. 3.5. Mode 2 is commonly used for setting baud rates for serial communication.

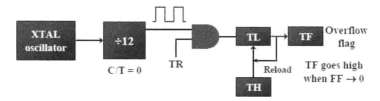

Figure 3.5: MODE 2

Q. Write an ALP to create a square wave of period $544.67\mu s$. Use Timer 1 in the auto reload mode.

```
        MOV TMOD,#20H
        MOV TH1,#0
        SETB TR1
BACK:JNB TF1,BACK
        CPL P1.0
        CLR TF1
        SJMP BACK
```

Q. Write an ALP to generate 1 KHz square wave on pin P1.2. Use Timer 0 in mode 2.
Maximum delay possible is $139\mu s$. Smallest frequency is $2 \times 139 = 278\mu s$. To get a delay of $0.5ms$, we need $0.5ms/0.546\mu s = 915$cycles. We use TH register to get a delay of 183 cycles and a register R0 to get the rest of it.
Use the formula defined earlier.

```
        MOV TMOD,#02H
REPT:   CPL P1.2
        MOV R0,#05
AGAIN:MOV TH0,#49H
        SETB TR0
BACK:   JNB TF0,BACK
        CLR TR0
        CLR TF0
        DJNZ R0,AGAIN
        SJMP REPT
```

3.4   Counter Programming

- In the counter mode, the timer is used for counting external events such as key presses, number of pulses of an external signal etc.

- C/T bit in TMOD decides the clock source for the timer.

- When C/T = 1, the timer is used as a counter and gets its pulses from outside the 8051

- The counter counts up as pulses are fed from pins 14 and 15, these pins are called T0 (timer 0 input) and T1 (timer 1 input)

Table 3.2: Port 3 Pins used for counter operation

Pin	Port Pin	Function	Description
14	P3.4	T0	Timer/counter 0 external input
15	P3.5	T1	Timer/counter 1 external input

Figure 3.6: Timer with external input (mode 1)

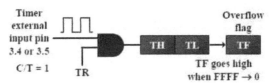

Q. Assuming that clock pulses are fed into pin T1, write a program for counter 1 in mode 2 to count the pulses and display the state of the TL1 count on P2, which connects to 8 LEDs.

21

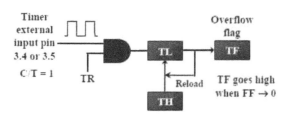

Figure 3.7: Timer with external input (mode 2)

```
       MOV TMOD,#01100000B ;counter 1, mode 2,
                  ;C/T=1 external pulses
       MOV TH1,#0 ;clear TH1
       SETB P3.5 ;make T1 input
AGAIN:SETB TR1 ;start the counter
BACK: MOV A,TL1 ;get copy of TL
       MOV P2,A ;display it on port 2
       JNB TF1,Back ;keep doing, if TF = 0
       CLR TR1 ;stop the counter 1
       CLR TF1 ;make TF=0
       SJMP AGAIN ;keep doing it
```

Since ports are set up for output when the 8051 is powered up, we make P3.5 an input port by making it high.

3.5   When GATE=1

- If GATE = 1, the start and stop of the timer are done externally through pins P3.2 and P3.3 for timers 0 and 1, respectively

- This hardware way allows to start or stop the timer externally at any time via a simple switch

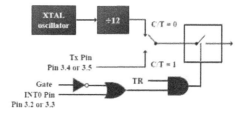

Figure 3.8: Timer/Counter 0, when GATE=1

22

Chapter 4

Interrupt Programming-The Prelude & Timer Interrupts

4.1 Introduction

4.1.1 Example from our day-to-day life

Suppose your mobile turns bad and it stops vibrating and ringing. Someone tells you that he will be calling you in an hour. What would you do? You will take out your mobile frequently, like once every 10 seconds to see if he has called. You keep on doing this every 10 seconds till he call you. This process is called polling. This isn't an efficient approach because you need to poll many times even though he hasn't called you. It wastes your time. And suppose, you checked your mobile at 1:00:00 pm and he calls you at 1:00:01 pm, you don't find it until the polling at 1:00:10 pm. Sometimes, that may not be appreciated. In the other way, if your mobile has some call alert system, you dont need to poll, when you hear the ringtone, you realise that he is calling. You have two advantages here, 1) you don't need to waste your time polling and 2) you know about the call at the same time his call has reached your mobile.

4.1.2 Formal introduction

- An **interrupt** is an event external to the currently executing process that causes a change in the normal flow of instruction execution; usually generated by hardware devices external to the CPU You prefer polling to interrupt when the event is

1. Asynchronous, you don't know when the event is going to happen.

2. Urgent, you cant wait for the CPU to poll other events and then poll for the current event in a round robin fashion.

3. Less frequent, if the event is highly frequent,polling will also be a better choice.

- In polling,

  - The microcontroller continuously monitors the status of a given device
  - When the conditions met, it performs the service
  - After that, it moves on to monitor the next device until every one is serviced

- In interrupt,

  - Whenever any device needs its service, the device notifies the microcontroller by sending it an interrupt signal
  - Upon receiving an interrupt signal, the microcontroller interrupts whatever it is doing and serves the device
  - The program which is associated with the interrupt is called the interrupt service routine (ISR) or interrupt handler

- Advantage of interrupt over polling is that in interrupt,

  - We can assign priority to interrupt and based on the priority, the interrupts will be handled.
  - It is possible to mask or ignore a request for service.

Interrupt	ROM Location (hex)	Pin
Reset	0000	9
External HW (INT0)	0003	P3.2 (12)
Timer 0 (TF0)	000B	
External HW (INT1)	0013	P3.3 (13)
Timer 1 (TF1)	001B	
Serial COM (RI and TI)	0023	

Figure 4.1: Interrupt vector table

24

- For every interrupt, there must be an ISR (Interrupt Service Routine) associated with it.

- The group of memory locations set aside to hold the addresses of ISRs is called interrupt vector table. This is shown in Fig. 4.1.

4.2   Steps in executing an interrupt

. Upon activation of an interrupt, the microcontroller goes through the following steps

1. It finishes the instruction it is executing and saves the address of the next instruction (PC) on the stack

2. It also saves the current status of all the interrupts internally (i.e: not on the stack)

3. It jumps to a fixed location in memory, called the interrupt vector table, that holds the address of the ISR.

4. The microcontroller gets the address of the ISR from the interrupt vector table and jumps to it

   - It starts to execute the interrupt service subroutine until it reaches the last instruction of the subroutine which is RETI (return from interrupt)

5. Upon executing the RETI instruction, the microcontroller returns to the place where it was interrupted

   - First, it gets the program counter (PC) address from the stack by popping the top two bytes of the stack into the PC
   - Then it starts to execute from that address

4.3   Interrupts in 8051

- Reset âĂŞ power-up reset.

- Two interrupts are set aside for the timers: one for timer 0 and one for timer 1.

- Two interrupts are set aside for hardware external interrupts.

- P3.2 and P3.3 are for the external hardware interrupts INT0, and INT1.

- Serial communication has a single interrupt that belongs to both receive and transfer.

4.4 Enabling and disabling interrupts

- Upon reset, all interrupts are disabled (masked), meaning that none will be responded to by the microcontroller if they are activated

- The interrupts must be enabled by software in order for the microcontroller to respond to them

- There is a register called IE (interrupt enable) that is responsible for enabling (unmasking) and disabling (masking) the interrupts

Figure 4.2: Interrupt Enable register

- IE ot **I**nterrupt **E**nable register is shown in Fig. 4.2.

- It is a bit addressable register.

  EA or **IE.7**: Disables all interrupts

  - or **IE.6**: Not implemented, reserved for future use

  ET2 or **IE.5**: Enables or disables timer 2 overflow (8052 only)

  ES or **IE.4**: Enables or disables the serial port interrupt

  ET1 or **IE.3**: Enables or disables timer 1 overflow interrupt

  EX1 or **IE.2**: Enables or disables external interrupt 1

  ET0 or **IE.1**: Enables or disables timer 0 overflow interrupt

  EX0 or **IE.0**: Enables or disables external interrupt 0

Exercise 4.1 *Show the instructions to*

(a) enable the serial interrupt, timer 0 interrupt, and external hardware interrupt 1 (EX1)

(b) disable (mask) the timer 0 interrupt,

(c) show how to disable all the interrupts with a single instruction.

Solution:

(a)
```
MOV IE,#10010110B ;enable serial, timer 0, EX1
Another way to perform the same manipulation is
SETB IE.7 ;EA=1, global enable
SETB IE.4 ;enable serial interrupt
SETB IE.1 ;enable Timer 0 interrupt
SETB IE.2 ;enable EX1
```

(b) CLR IE.1 ;mask (disable) timer 0 ;interrupt only

(c) CLR IE.7 ;disable all interrupts

4.5 Timer interrupts

The timer flag (TF) is raised when the timer rolls over

- In polling TF, we have to wait until the TF is raised

  - The problem with this method is that the microcontroller is tied down while waiting for TF to be raised, and can not do anything else

- Using interrupts solves this problem and, avoids tying down the controller

  - If the timer interrupt in the IE register is enabled, whenever the timer rolls over, TF is raised, and the microcontroller is interrupted in whatever it is doing, and jumps to the interrupt vector table to service the ISR

  - In this way, the microcontroller can do other until it is notified that the timer has rolled over

27

Exercise

Exercise 4.2 *Write a program that displays a value of 'Y' at port 0 and 'N' at port 2 ans also generate a square wave of 10 KHz with timer 0 in mode 2 at port pin P1.2. $XTAL = 22MHz$*

Solution:

```
        ORG 0000H
        LJMP MAIN;   bypass interrupt vecotr table
    ;  ISR doe timer 0 to generate sqaure wave
        ORG 000BH
        CPL P1.2
        RETI
    ;  the main program
        ORG 0030H
MAIN:  MOV TMOD, #02H; timer 0, mode 2 (autp-reload)
        MOV TH0, #0B6H
        MOV IE, #82H; enable interrupt timer 0
        SETB TR0; start timer 0
BACK:  MOV P0, #'Y'
        MOV P2, #'N'
        SJMP BACK
        END
```

28

Exercise

Exercise 4.3 *Write a program to generate two square waves- one of 5 Khz frequency at pin P1.3 and another of frequency 25 KHz at pin P2.3. Assume* $XTAL = 22MHz$

Solution:

```
        ORG 0000H
        LJMP MAIN;  bypass interrupt vecotr table
     ; ISR doe timer 0
        ORG 000BH
        CPL P1.3
        RETI
     ; ISR doe timer 1
        ORG 001BH
        CPL P2.3
        RETI
     ; the main program
        ORG 0030H
MAIN:  MOV TMOD, #22H; timer 0, mode 2 (auto-reload)
        MOV IE, #8AH; enable interrupt timer 0 and timer 1
        MOV TH0, #048H; 5 KHz
        MPOV TH1, #0DBH; 25KHz
        SET TR0
        SET TR1
WAIT:  SJMP WAIT
        END
```

Exercise 4.4 *Write a program to toggle pin P1.2 every second. Assume* $XTAL = 22MHz$

Solution:

To get a delay of 1sec, we need to use a register, in addition to a timer. R0 is used along with Timer 1 to get a large delay.

```
        ORG 0000H
        LJMP MAIN;  bypass interrupt vecotr table
    ; ISR doe timer 1
        ORG 001BH
        DJNZ R0, START
        CPL P1.2
        MOV R0, #28
        MOV TL1, #00H
        MOV TH1,#00H
        RETI
    ; the main program
        ORG 0030H
MAIN: MOV TMOD, #10H; timer 1, mode 1
        MOV IE, #88H; enable interrupt timer 1
        MOV R0, #28H
        MOV TL1, #00H
        MOV TH1, #00H
        SET TR1
WAIT: SJMP WAIT
        END
```

Exercise

Exercise 4.5 *Write a program to generate a square wave if 50Hz frequency on pin P1.2. This is similar to Example 9-12 except that it uses an interrupt for timer 0. Assume that $XTAL = 11.0592MHz$*

Solution:

```
        ORG 0
        LJMP MAIN
        ORG 000BH ;ISR for Timer 0
        CPL P1.2
        MOV TL0,#00
        MOV TH0,#0DCH
        RETI
        ORG 30H
;————main program for initialization
MAIN:MOV TM0D,#00000001B ;Timer 0, Mode 1
        MOV TL0,#00
        MOV TH0,#0DCH
        MOV IE,#82H ;enable Timer 0 interrupt
        SETB TR0
HERE:SJMP HERE
        END
```

Chapter 5

External Interrupts and Prelude to Serial Communication

5.1 External interrupts

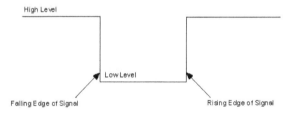

Figure 5.1: Level and edge

- Fig.5.1 shows different possible triggers.

- 8051 has two external interrupts.

- They are INT0, located on P3.2 and INT1 on P3.3.

- Interrupt vector table locations are 0003H for INT0 and 0013H for INT1.

- External interrupts can be enabled or disabled using the IE register as with the case of other interrupts.

- There are two types of activation for the interrupts:

    1. level triggered

2. edge triggered

5.1.1   Level-triggered/Level-activated triggered interrupt

1. Normally, the interrupt pin will be high.

2. For low level triggering of the interrupt, we feed a low signal to the interrupt.

3. Once an interrupt is triggered, the microcontroller finishes the instruction it is executing and moves to the corresponding ISR, as mentioned in Section 4.2.

4. The last instruction in the ISR is *RETI*. The interrupt should be removed before the execution of this instruction, else the interrupt will be re-triggered.

Exercise 5.1 *Assume that the common terminal of a single pole double throw switch is connected to the INT1 of a microcontroller. One contact is connected to the ground and the other to supply voltage through a resistor as shown in the figure. Write an assembly language program to turn ON the led by using the switch. The light should stay turned ON for a fraction of seconds even after releasing the switch. Assume that the LED is connected in such a way that it is ON when P1.2 is made high.*

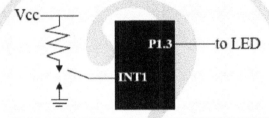

<u>Solution:</u>

```
       ORG 0000H
       LJMP MAIN
;--ISR for INT1 to turn on LED
       ORG 0013H ;INT1 ISR
       SETB P1.3 ;turn on LED
       MOV R0,#255
  BACK:DJNZ R0,BACK ;delay
       CLR P1.3 ;turn off the LED
       RETI ;return from ISR
;--MAIN program for initialization
       ORG 30H
  MAIN:MOV IE,#10000100B ;enable external INT 1
  HERE:SJMP HERE ;stay here until get interrupted
       END
```

Sampling the low level-triggered interrupt

- The duration of the interrupt shouldn't be too short or too long. If it is too short, an interrupt may not be triggered. If it is too long, interrupt will be re triggered. This has certainly to be avoided.

- The interrupt should be long enough so that the pin is held low until the start of the execution of the interrupt. This typically takes 4 machine cycles, hence the interrupt should be held low for 4 machine cycles because

34

- If the INTx pin is low after the RETI instruction of the ISR another interrupt will be triggered after the one instruction is executed.

- The interrupt has to be held high for at least 4 machine cycles because the level-triggered interrupt is not latched.

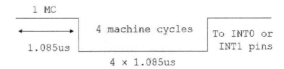

Figure 5.2: Ideal duration for low level triggered interrupt

- The ideal duration for low level triggered interrupt is shown in Fig.5.2.

5.1.2 Edge-triggered interrupts

- Upon reset, the external interrupts of 8051 will be level triggered.

- To make them edge triggered, we need to modify the IT0 (D0 or TCON.0) and IT1 (D2 or TCON.2) bits of the TCON register.

- When ITx is '0', the interrupt will be level triggered and when '1' it will be edge triggered (H-L transition).

- Edge triggered interrupt is latched by the IEx flags of the TCON register.

Exercise 5.2 *Write an ALP to generate a square wave at pin P0.0. The frequency of the square wave should be half of the frequency of the signal applied at pin P3.3 (INT1).*

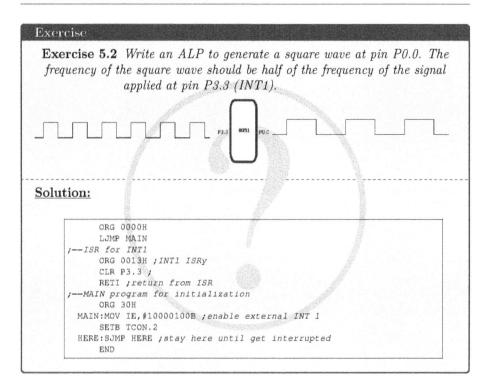

Solution:

```
        ORG 0000H
        LJMP MAIN
;--ISR for INT1
        ORG 0013H ;INT1 ISRy
        CLR P3.3 ;
        RETI ;return from ISR
;--MAIN program for initialization
        ORG 30H
MAIN:MOV IE,#10000100B ;enable external INT 1
        SETB TCON.2
HERE:SJMP HERE ;stay here until get interrupted
        END
```

Sampling the edge-triggered interrupt

- For getting triggered by an edge-trigger interrupt, the external source must be held high for one machine cycle and low for the next machine cycle. (Remember, the interrupt should be a High-Low transition.)

- The falling edge is latched by the IEx bits of the TCON register. TCON.1/IE0 is for INT0 and TCON.2/IE1 is for INT1.

- Once an interrupt is latched, i.e., IEx is set, the microcontroller will not respond to any new interrupts on the INTx pin until the flag is cleared. Hence, IEx are also known as the *interrupt-in-service flags.*

- The RETI instruction in the ISR will clear the IEx.

- For a fresh triggering of the interrupt, the external signal must go from high to low.

Exercise 5.3 *What is the difference between RET instruction and RETI instruction?*

Answer:

Both RET and RETI pops out the two bytes from the stack and load them into the program counter so that the mircrontroller can move back to where it left off. But **RETI does the additional task of clearing the interrupt service flag** so that the microcontroller can accept further interrupts. Instead, if RET is used, the flags will not be cleared and hence after the first interrupt, the microcontroller will not respond to further interrupts. This is true for both the timer interrupts and the external interrupts but **not for serial interrupt**.

5.2 Serial Communication

5.2.1 Serial v/s parallel communication

May 2012, KU

Serial communication is preferred due to the following reasons:
Serial communication

- has reduced cabling cost

- requires smaller connectors

- reduced effects of clock skew

- reduced effects of crosstalk

Parallel communication offers higher speed if crosstalk and clock skew are eliminated.

5.2.2 Communication strategies

- **Asynchronous communication:** In asynchronous communication. data is transferred as a single byte at a time.

- **Synchronous communication:** In synchronous communication, data is transmitted as block of data (character) at a time.

37

- There are special ICs for both:

    - UART: Universal **A**synchronous **R**eceiver **T**ransmitter
    - USART: Universal **S**ynchronous **A**synchronous **R**eceiver **T**ransmitter

Serial data transfers depend on accurate timing in order to differentiate bits in the data stream. This timing can be handled in one of two ways: asynchronously or synchronously. In asynchronous communication, the scope of the timing is a single byte. In synchronous communication, the timing scope comprises one or more blocks of bytes. The terms asynchronous and synchronous are slightly misleading, because both kinds of communication require synchronization between the sender and receiver. Asynchronous communication is the prevailing standard in the personal computer industry, both because it is easier to implement and because it has the unique advantage that bytes can be sent whenever they are ready, as opposed to waiting for blocks of data to accumulate.

Asynchronous means "no synchronization", and thus does not require sending and receiving idle characters. However, the beginning and end of each byte of data must be identified by start and stop bits. The start bit indicates when the data byte is about to begin and the stop bit signals when it ends. The requirement to send these additional two bits cause asynchronous communications to be slightly slower than synchronous however it has the advantage that the processor does not have to deal with the additional idle characters.

Source: `http://www.pccompci.com`

Advantages and disadvantages of asynchronous communication

- **Advantages**

    Simple since no synchronisation at both sides is required.

    Cheaper than synchronous communication due to the reduction in the hardware cost.

    Can be set-up faster than synchronous communication.

- **Disadvantages**

    Larger overhead

    Lower throughput

Advantages and disadvantages of synchronous communication

- **Advantages**

  Lower overhead

  Higher throughput

- **Disadvantages**

  More complex

  More expensive

5.2.3 Transmission modes

May 2012, KU

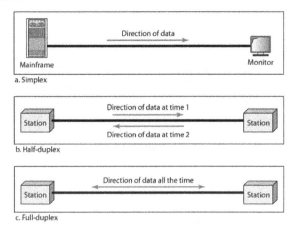

Figure 5.3: Modes of channel operation. Source:www.tauruscodespot.blogspot.com

- **Simplex:** In simplex mode of channel operation, data transmission can happen in one predefined direction only.
  eg.: Radio broadcast

- **Half duplex:** In this mode, data can be transmitted in both direction but not at the same time.
  eg.: handheld transceiver (walkie-talkie)

- **Full duplex:** In this mode, data can travel in both directions simultaneously.
  eg.: landline telephone

5.2.4 Data framing

- In asynchronous transmission, both the transmitter and receiver agrees upon a set of rules known as the **protocol**. The protocol defines:

  1. How the data is packed
  2. The nature and number of start and stop bits
  3. How many bits constitute a character
  4. Type of the error correction/error detection rule, if any.

- When the line is idle, the signal transmitted is 1 or high. This is referred to as **"mark"**. "Mark" indicated that the communication link is up and running.

- The low signal is referred to as **"space"**. Transition from "mark to space" indicates that an event is occurring, either the link is getting interrupted or a data is going to be transited.

- Transition from "mark" to "space" for a predefined time called the **bit time** indicates that a data is going to be transmitted. This "space" is referred to as the **"start bit"**.

- The LSB is transmitted first.

- After the MSB, a stop bit, which is a high signal is transferred indicating the end of data.

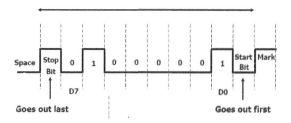

Figure 5.4: Data framing: 'A', 8-bit ASCII

- An example of data framing is shown in Fig. 5.4.

- In older systems, instead of one stop bit, two stop bits were used to give the mechanical devices sufficient time before the transmission of the next byte.

- Assume that we are using extended ASCII (8-bit), we will have two overhead bits (start and stop bits) per byte. Hence the total overhead is 25%.

- For error detection, some systems employ an extra bit called the parity bit in the data frame.

  Odd parity: Parity bit is '1' if the number of 1's including the parity bit is odd.

  even parity: Parity bit is '1' if the number of 1's including the parity bit is even.

- For eg., ASCII character 'A' (0100 0001 B) has '0' for the even parity bit.

5.2.5 Data transfer rate

- Typical unit for data rate is *bps* or "bits per second".

- Another commonly used unit is "baud rate". Baud rate is defined as the number of signal changes per second.

- Baud rate and bps are not necessarily equal because in modern systems, a single signal change can transfer several bits of data.

5.2.6 RS232 Standards

- To make the different data communication equipments compatible to each other, an interfacing standard, called **RS232** was developed by the **E**lectronics **I**ndustries **A**ssociation (EIA) in 1960.

- This was later modified as *RS232A* (1963), *RS232B* (1953) and *RS232C* (1969).

- Since these standards were developed before the advent of TTL technology, RS232 isn't TTL compatible.

- In RS232, '1' is represented by -3V to -25V and '0' by 3V to 25V, making -3V to +3V undefined.

- Therefore to connect RS232 to a microcontroller, we need to convert the TTL voltage levels to RS232 voltage levels and vice versa.

- For this purpose, we use IC chips known as "line drivers" like the MAX232.

41

5.2.7 RS232 pins

Table 5.1: RS232 DB-25 pin description

Pin	Description	Pin	Description
1	Protective ground	14	Secondary transmitted data
2	Transmitted data (TxD)	15	Transmitted signal element timing
3	Received data (RxD)	16	Secondary receive data
4	Request to send (-RTS)	17	Receive signal element timing
5	Clear to send (-CTS)	18	Unassigned
6	Data set ready (-DSR)	19	Secondary receive data
7	Signal ground (GND)	20	Data terminal ready (-DTR)
8	Data carrier detect (-DCD)	21	Signal quality detector
9/10	Reserved for data testing	22	Ring indicator (RI)
11	Unassigned	23	Data signal rate select
12	Secondary data carrier detect	24	Transmit signal element timing
13	Secondary clear to send	25	Unassigned

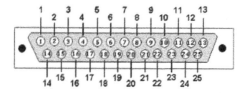

Figure 5.5: DB-25 connector

- Table 5.1 gives the pin description of a RS232 cable.

- RS232 is commonly referred to as the DB-25 connector.

- DB-25P is the plug connector (male) and DB-25S is the socket connector (female).

- Fig. 5.5 shows a DB-25 connector.

42

Pin	Description
1	Data carrier detect (-DCD)
2	Received data (RxD)
3	Transmitted data (TxD)
4	Data terminal ready (DTR)
5	Signal ground (GND)
6	Data set ready (-DSR)
7	Request to send (-RTS)
8	Clear to send (-CTS)
9	Ring indicator (RI)

Figure 5.6: DB-9 connector

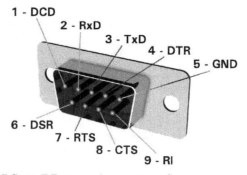

Figure 5.7: RS232 DB-9 pin description. Source: www.ethernut.de

Since not all pins are used, IBM introduced the DB-9 version which has only 9 pins. This is shown in Fig. 5.7. The pins description is given in Table 5.6.

5.2.8 Data communication classification

- Data communication equipments can be classified into two:

    1. **DTE:** Data Terminal Equipments are terminals and computers that send and receive data.

    2. **DCE:** Data Communication Equipments are communication equipments such as modems that are responsible for transferring the data.

43

5.2.9   8051 connection to RS232

RxD and TxD pins in the 8051

- There are two dedicated pins in 80512 for transmitting and receiving data serially.

- They are:

  - TxD (Pin 11/ P3.1 of port 3): For transmitting data.
  - RxD (Pin 10/ P3.0 of port 3): For receiving data.

- Since the TxD and RxD ports of 8051 are TTL compatible and RS232 isn't TTL compatible, we need to use a line driver like MAX232 for interfacing 8051 with RS232.

5.2.10   MAX232

- As discussed earlier, we need to use line drivers for converting RS232 voltage levels to TTL voltage levels and vice versa.

- MAX232 uses a +5V power source, which is the same source for the 8051.

- That is, a single power supply can power both 8051 and MAX232, no need for dual power supply.

- We have two sets of line drivers in MAX232; T1 and T2 used for TxD and R1 and R2 used for RxD.

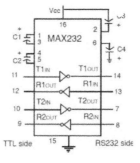

Figure 5.8: Internal diagram of MAX232

44

- As shown in Fig.5.8, pin 11 and pin 10 are respectively designated as "T1in" and "T1out".

- T1in pin is the TTL side and is connected to the TxD of the microcontroller, while T1out is the RS232 side, connected to the RS232 DB connector.

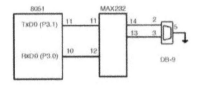

Figure 5.9: RS232 to 80512

- Similarly, for the R1 driver as shown in Fig. 5.9.

5.2.11 Basic of 8051 serial port programming

- 8051 supports many baud rates.

- Different baud rates can be achieved using timer 1.

- Usually, for generating baud rate, timer 1 is set in mode1 (auto reload mode).

- The 80512 microcontroller divides crystal frequency by 12 before it is fed to the timer.

Figure 5.10: Generation of frequency for setting baud rate

- This value is again divided by 32 by the UART as shown in Fig.5.10.

5.2.12 Steps to calculate the value to be loaded into TH1 for a given baud rate

1. Let b be the given baud rate and c be the crystal frequency

45

2. Then, the frequency of the signal fed to the Timer 1 for setting baud rate is

$$f = \frac{c}{32 \times 12} \qquad (5.1)$$

3. Let $v = \frac{f}{b}$

4. Take the negative of v and load this decimal value into TH1 using the instruction

```
MOV TH1,#-v D
```

Exercise

Exercise 5.4 *Find the value to be loaded into TH1 for obtaining a baud rate of 9600 Bd. Assume XTAL frequency is 11.0592 MHz*

Solution:

1. $b = 9600$ and $c = 11.0592 MHz$

2. $f = \frac{11.0592 MHz}{32 \times 12} = 28800 Hx$

3. $v = \frac{28800}{9600} = 3$

4. $-v = -3D = FDH$

5. MOV TH1, #-3 D

For other baud rates,

Baud Rate	TH1 (Decimal)	TH1 (Hex)
4800	-6	FA
2400	-12	F4
1200	-24	E8

46

Chapter 6

Serial Port Programming

6.1 Special purpose registers

6.1.1 SBUF Register

- 8 bit register used exclusively for serial communication

- To transfer a byte via serial communication, it has to be placed in the SBUF register.

  Once a byte is placed, in the SBUF, 8051 frames it with the start bit and the stop bit and transfers the data through TxD pin.

- Serial data received from the RxD line of 8051 is stored in the SBUF register.

  Once a data is received, 8051 deframes it by removing the start bit and the stop bit.

6.1.2 SCON (Serial CONtrol register)

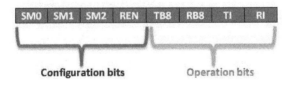

Figure 6.1: SCON register

- 8 bit register as shown in Fig.6.1.

- The first 4 bits (SCON.4-SCON.7) are the configuration bits.

Table 6.1: Serial port modes

SM0	SM1	Serial Mode	Explanation	Baud Rate
0	0	0	8 bit shift register	Oscillator/12
0	1	1	8-bit UART	Set by timer 1
1	0	2	9-bit UART	Oscillator/64
1	1	3	9-bit UART	Set by timer 1

- **SM0** and **SM1** are for specifying serial port mode. Various modes are shown in Table 6.1.

- The baud rate of modes 1,2 &3 doubles if PCON.7 (SMOD) is set.

- **SM2** is for multiporcessor communication. If set, the RI flag will not be set even if the 9th bit of the received data is '1'.

- **REN** or **R**eceive **EN**able should be set for receiving data via the serial pin RxD.

- The last 4 bits, (SCON.0-SCON.3) are hte operational bits, used during the operation of the serial port.

- **TB8** is used in modes 2 and 3. The last bit (9th) of the transmitted data will be the content TB0.

- **RB8** is used in modes 2 and 3. The 9th bit of the received data will be the content RB8.

- **TI** is the **T**ransmit **I**nterrupt flag, set by the hardware at the beginning of the stop bit in mode 1. This lets the program know that the byte has be transferred and the serial port is ready for another transmission. TI flag must be cleared manually for the next transmission.

- **RI** is the **R**eceive **I**nterrupt flag, set by the hardware halfway through the stop bit time in mode 1. RI flag must be cleared manually for the next reception.

6.1.3   PCON Power CONtrol register

Figure 6.2: PCON register

- PCON register is shown in Fig. 6.2.

- If the last bit **SMOD** is '0', the crystal frequency is divided by 12 followed by **32** for setting the baud rate.

- If set, the crystal frequency is divided by 12 followed by **16** for setting the baud rate.

- PCON is not bit addressable. One way to set SMOD alone is,

```
MOV A,PCON
SETB PCON.7
MOV PCON,A
```

6.2   Steps for serial reception

1. Load TMOD with $20H$, which corresponds to Timer 1 in mode-2

2. Load the appropriate value into TH1.

3. Load SCON with the value $50H$, which corresponds to serial mode 1.

4. Set TR1 to start timer 1.

5. Clear RI for enabling serial reception.

6. Monitor RI flag using the instruction "JNB Ri".

7. If RI is raised, it means that the entire byte has been received and is stored in SBUF.

8. Go to **5** for receiving the next byte.

49

Exercise 6.1 *Write a program for the 8051 to receive bytes of data serially, and put them in P1, set the baud rate at 4800, 8-bit data, and 1 stop bit*

Solution:

```
        MOV TMOD,#20H ;timer 1,mode 2(auto reload)
        MOV TH1,#-6 ;4800 baud rate
        MOV SCON,#50H ;8-bit, 1 stop, REN enabled
        SETB TR1 ;start timer 1
HERE:   JNB RI,HERE ;wait for char to come in
        MOV A,SBUF ;saving incoming byte in A
        MOV P1,A ;send to port 1
        CLR RI ;get ready to receive next byte
        SJMP HERE ;keep getting data
```

6.3 Steps for serial transmission

1. Load TMOD with $20H$, which corresponds to Timer 1 in mode-2

2. Load the appropriate value into TH1.

3. Load SCON with the value $50H$, which corresponds to serial mode 1.

4. Set TR1 to start timer 1.

5. Clear TI for enabling serial reception.

6. Write the data to be transferred into SBUF.

7. Monitor TI flag.

8. Go to **5** for transferring the next byte.

Exercise 6.2 *Write a program for the 8051 to transfer "CET" serially at 9600 baud, 8-bit data, 1 stop bit, do this continuously.*

Solution:

```
        MOV TMOD,#20H ;timer 1,mode 2(auto reload)
        MOV TH1,#-3 ;9600 baud rate
        MOV SCON,#50H ;8-bit, 1 stop, REN enabled
        SETB TR1 ;start timer 1
AGAIN:MOV A,#  C    ;transfer    C
        ACALL TRANS
        MOV A,#  E    ;transfer    E
        ACALL TRANS
        MOV A,#  T    ;transfer    T
        ACALL TRANS
        SJMP AGAIN ;keep doing it
;serial data transfer subroutine
TRANS:MOV SBUF,A ;load SBUF
HERE:JNB TI,HERE ;wait for the last bit
        CLR TI ;get ready for next byte
        RET
```

Chapter 7

The ARM Run Through

7.1   RISC v/s CISC

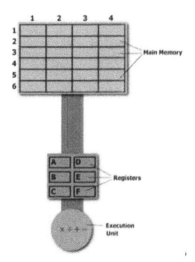

Figure 7.1: Storage system. Source: `http://cs.stanford.edu/` &Arstechnica

Consider the storage scheme of a generic computer shown in Fig. 7.1. Assume that the execution unit can operate only on the data loaded into one of the six registers (A,B,...F). Suppose we want to multiply two elements in the memory, say the data in location [3,4] and [1,2] and store the result in [1,2]. In a CISC based architecture, the goal is to complete the given task using as few assembly instructions as possible. So, it will have a specific instruction, say "MUL" which can fetch the data from memory, store it in the registers, do the multiplication operation and store back the results.

In CISC, the instruction can be,

MUL [1,2],[3,4].

What is so good here is that the assembly code is simple, more like a high-level code, uses less RAM for storing instruction but the hardware should be able to interpret this instruction, make it complex.

But in a RISC based computer, the instruction are simple in nature and they take only one clock cycle for execution. SO the "MUL" instruction defined will be split into several stages such as LOAD, MULT and STORE as given below,

    LOAD A,[3,4]

    LOAD B,[1,2]

    MULT A,B

    STORE [1,2],A

All instruction execute in a single cycle and hence pipelining is possible. Also, less hardware is required in RISC. To summarise,

CISC	RISC
Emphasis on hardware	Emphasis on software
Includes multi-clock complex instructions	Single-clock, reduced instruction only
Memory-to-memory: "LOAD" and "STORE" incorporated in instructions	Register to register: "LOAD" and "STORE" are independent instructions
Small code sizes, high cycles per second	Low cycles per second, large code sizes
Transistors used for storing complex instructions	Spends more transistors on memory registers

7.2 ARM Data types

The ARM processor supports the following data types:

1. words, 32-bit

2. halfwords, 16-bit

3. bytes, 8-bit.

7.3 Operating modes

The ARM processor has seven modes of operation:

1. User mode is the usual ARM program execution state, and is used for executing most application programs.

2. Fast Interrupt (FIQ) mode supports a data transfer or channel process.

3. Interrupt (IRQ) mode is used for general-purpose interrupt handling.

4. Supervisor mode is a protected mode for the operating system.

5. Abort mode is entered after a data or instruction Prefetch Abort.

6. System mode is a privileged user mode for the operating system. System mode can be entered from another privileged mode by modifying the mode bit of the Current Program Status Register (CPSR).

7. Undefined mode is entered when an undefined instruction is executed.

Table 7.1: Mode identifiers

Mode	Mode identifier
User	*usr*
Fast interrupt	*fiq*
Interrupt	*irq*
Supervisor	*svc*
Abort	*abt*
System	*sys*
Undefined	*und*

Each mode has an identifier as shown in Table 7.1.

7.4 Registers

ARM has a total of 37 registers,

1. 31 general purpose registers which are of 32 bits width

2. 6 status registers

54

In ARM state, 16 general registers and one or two status registers are accessible at any one time. In privileged modes, mode-specific banked registers become available.

The ARM-state register set contains 16 directly-accessible registers, r0 to r15. A further register, the CPSR, contains condition code flags and the current mode bits. Registers r0 to r13 are general-purpose registers used to hold either data or address values. Registers r14 and r15 have the following special functions: Link register

Register r14 is used as the subroutine Link Register (LR). Register r14 receives a copy of r15 when a Branch with Link (BL) instruction is executed. At all other times we can treat r14 as a general-purpose register. The corresponding banked registers r14_svc, r14_irq, r14_fiq, r14_abt and r14_und are similarly used to hold the return values of r15 when interrupts and exceptions arise, or when BL instructions are executed within interrupt or exception routines. Program counter Register r15 holds the PC. By convention, r13 is used as the Stack Pointer (SP).

In privileged modes, another register, the Saved Program Status Register (SPSR), is accessible. This contains the condition code flags and the mode bits saved as a result of the exception which caused entry to the current mode.

Banked registers are discrete physical registers in the core that are mapped to the available registers depending on the current processor operating mode. Banked register contents are preserved across operating mode changes. FIQ mode has seven banked registers mapped to r8âĂŞr14 (r8_fiqâĂŞr14_fiq). In ARM state, many FIQ handlers do not have to save any registers. The User, IRQ, Supervisor, Abort, and undefined modes each have two banked registers mapped to r13 and r14, allowing a private SP and LR for each mode. System mode shares the same registers as User mode.

These are shown in Fig.7.2.

System and User	FIQ	Supervisor	Abort	IRQ	Undefined
r0	r0	r0	r0	r0	r0
r1	r1	r1	r1	r1	r1
r2	r2	r2	r2	r2	r2
r3	r3	r3	r3	r3	r3
r4	r4	r4	r4	r4	r4
r5	r5	r5	r5	r5	r5
r6	r6	r6	r6	r6	r6
r7	r7	r7	r7	r7	r7
r8	r8_fiq	r8	r8	r8	r8
r9	r9_fiq	r9	r9	r9	r9
r10	r10_fiq	r10	r10	r10	r10
r11	r11_fiq	r11	r11	r11	r11
r12	r12_fiq	r12	r12	r12	r12
r13	r13_fiq	r13_svc	r13_abt	r13_irq	r13_und
r14	r14_fiq	r14_svc	r14_abt	r14_irq	r14_und
r15 (PC)	r15 (PC)	r15 (PC)	r15 (PC)	r15 (PC)	r15 (PC)

CPSR	CPSR	CPSR	CPSR	CPSR	CPSR
	SPSR_fiq	SPSR_svc	SPSR_abt	SPSR_irq	SPSR_und

= banked register

Figure 7.2: ARM registers

7.5 Program status word register

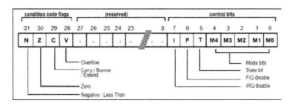

Figure 7.3: PSR

Program status register format is shown in Fig.7.3. Various modes are:

56

- Abort: 10111

- Fast interrupt request: 10001

- Interrupt request: 10010

- Supervisor: 10011

- System: 11111

- Undefined: 11011

- User: 10000

7.6 Interrupts

7.6.1 SWI, IRQ & FIQ

- Software interrupts are normally reserved to call privileged operating system routines, for eg.: for moving from *user* mode to a privileged mode.

- Interrupt Requests are normally assigned for general purpose interrupts.

- Fast Interrupt Requests are normally reserved for a single source that requires a fast response time.

7.6.2 Steps in interrupts handling

- The processor changes to a specific interrupt request mode, which reflects the interrupt being raised.

- The previous mode's cpsr is saved into the spsr of the new interrupt request mode.

- The pc is saved in the lr of the new interrupt request mode.

- Interrupts are disabled for preventing another interrupt of the same type begin raised.

- The processor branches to a specific entry in the vector table.

Exercise 7.1 *Fill the table for the full segment of code for ARM processor*

	r0=0X0	r1=0X1	r2=0XA	r3=0XF
UMLAL r0,r1,r2,r3				
RSB r0,r2,r2,LSL #3				
MOV r1,r0, ROR r2				
BIC r0,r3,r2				
CLZ r1,r2				
TST r3,r0				

Solution:

1. Unsigned Multiply Accumulate Long [r0,r1]=(r2*r3)+[r1,r0]

2. Reverse SuBtract and Logic Shift Left. r0=0X50-0XA

3. Rotate the content of r0 to right by the value in r2 (10 times) and store in r1

4. Logical bit clear (AND NOT)

5. count leading zeros

6. test for bits

	r0=0X0	r1=0X1	r2=0XA	r3=0XF
UMLAL r0,r1,r2,r3	0X96			
RSB r0,r2,r2,LSL #3	0X46			
MOV r1,r0, ROR r2	0X46	0X0		
BIC r0,r3,r2	0X5			
CLZ r1,r2		0X1C		
TST r3,r0				

Chapter 8

ARM Interrupts

8.1 Interrupt latency

- Defined as the time between an interrupt signal being raised and the fetch of the first instruction in the ISR of the instruction.

- Interrupt latency can be decreased by

    By allowing nested interrupt handling so that the system can respond to a new interrupt while handling an earlier interrupt. This is achieved by re-enabling interrupts while in the interrupt handler.

- But in this, interrupts will have latencies irrespective of their importance. Suppose we are servicing an interrupt and two interrupts having priorities higher than the present interrupt are raised, out of which one has higher priority than the other. Now if interrupts are served without considering the priorities, the highest priority interrupt may be serviced after the lower priority, thus increasing its latency. This can be prevented by servicing interrupts based on priorities.

Nested interrupt is given in Fig.8.1.

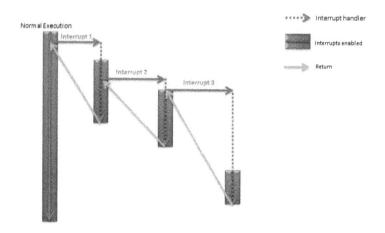

Figure 8.1: Nested interrupts

8.2 Interrupt handling schemes

Various interrupt handling schemes are:

1. **Nonnested interrupt handler:** Handles and services individual interrupts sequentially.

2. **Nested interrupted handler:** Handles multiple interrupts without a priority assignment.

3. **Reentrant interrupt handler:**Handles multiple interrupts that can be prioritized.

4. **Prioritizes simple interrupt handler:** Handles prioritizes interrupts.

5. **Prioritized standard interrupt handler:** Handles higer priority interrupts in a shorter time than lower priority interrupts.

6. **Prioritized direct interrupt handler:** Handles higher priority interrupts in a shorter time and goes directly to a specific service routine.

7. **Prioritized group interrupt handler:** Handles interrupts that are grouped into different priority levels.

8. **VIC PL190 based interrupt service routine:** Uses the Vector Interrupt Controller.

8.2.1   Nonnested interrupt handler

- Simplest interrupt handler

- Interrupts are disabled until control is returned back to the interrupted task.

- Can service only a single interrupt at a time.

- Not suitable for complex systems where multiple interrupts need to be serviced.

The various stages that occure when a system that has implemented a nonnested interrupt handler is interrupted are:

1. **Disable interrupts:** The processor will disable further interrupts from occurring since the system can handle only one interrupt at a time. It then switches to the appropriate interrupt request mode. The *cpsr* is copied to the newly available *spsr_mode*. The LR is stored with the PC value. Remember, $PC-8$ is the current instruction being executed and $PC-4$ is the instruction being decoded.

2. **Save context:** The handler saves a subset of the current processor mode nonbanked registers.

3. **Interrupt handler:** The handler then identifies the external interrupt source and executed the appropriate ISR.

4. **Interrupt service routine:** The ISR services the external interrupt source and resets the interrupt.

5. **Restore context:** The ISR returns back to the handler, which restores the context.

6. **Enable interrupts:** The *cpsr* is restored from *spsr_mode*. PC is loaded with $LR-4$.

This is shown in Fig. 8.2.

8.2.2   Summary

- Nonnested interrupt handler handles and services individual interrupts sequentially.

- High interrupt latency, cannot handle further interrupts while an interrupt is being serviced.

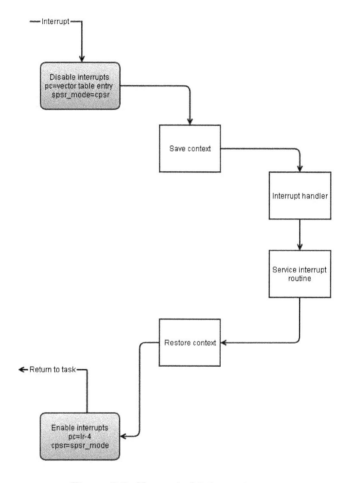

Figure 8.2: Nonnested interrupts

- **Advantages:** relatively easy to implement and debug.

- **Disadvantage:** cannot be used to handle complex embedded systems with multiple priority interrupts.

8.3 Nested interrupt handler

- Allows another interrupt to occur within the currently called handler. This is achieved by reenabling the interrupts before the handler has fully serviced the current interrupt.

- The first goal of any nested interrupt handler is to respond to interrupts quickly so that the handler neither waits for asynchronous exceptions, nor forces them to wait for the handler. The second goal is that execution of regular synchronous code is not delayed while servicing the various interrupts.

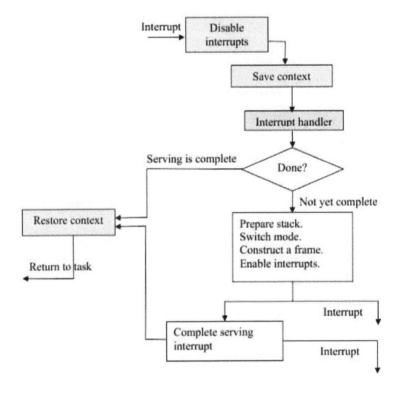

Figure 8.3: Nested interrupts. source: http://www.iti.uni-stuttgart.de

The various stages that occure when a system that has implemented a nested interrupt handler is interrupted are:

1. **Disable interrupts**

2. **Save context**

3. **Service interrupt:** ISR services the interrupt. The control is passes back to the handler when the servicing is complete or partially complete. TO indicate whether the servicing has completed or not, a flag is set or cleared. This flag is tested by the handler.If the flag indicates that the servicing is complete, the handler restores the context and returns to the suspended task. Else, further processing is required.

4. Stack is prepared.

5. Since interrupts cannot be enabled in the *IRQ* mode, the mode is changed to *SVC* or *System* mode.

6. All registers of the *IRQ* stack must be transferred to the task's stack. They are transferred to the reserved block of memory in the stack called *stack frame*.

7. Once in the *SVC* or *System* mode, the interrupts are reenabled and servicing is completed. During this time, the system may be again interrupted.

This is shown in Fig.8.3.

Bibliography

[1] "8051 addressing modes," Accessed: Nov. 11, 2013. [Online]. Available: http://www.circuitstoday.com/8051-addressing-modes

[2] M. A. Mazidi, J. G. Mazidi, and R. D. McKinlay, *The 8051 microcontroller and embedded systems: using Assembly and C.* Pearson/Prentice Hall, 2006, vol. 626.

[3] D. Calcutt, F. Cowan, and H. Parchizadeh, *8051 Microcontroller: An Applications Based Introduction.* Newnes, 2003.

[4] I. S. MacKenzie and R. C.-W. Phan, *The 8051 microcontroller.* Prentice Hall, 1999, vol. 3.

[5] K. J. Ayala *et al.*, *Eighty Fifty-One Microcontroller: Architecture, Programming, and Applications.* West Publishing Co., 1991.

[6] "RISC architecture," Accessed: Dec. 15, 2013. [Online]. Available: http://cs.stanford.edu/people/eroberts/courses/soco/projects/risc/risccisc/

[7] A. F. Abdelrazek, "Exception and interrupt handling in ARM," 2006.

[8] A. Sloss, D. Symes, and C. Wright, *ARM system developer's guide: designing and optimizing system software.* Morgan Kaufmann, 2004.